Best of Friends

The yearbook of Creative Monochrome

Editor
Roger Maile ARPS

CREATIVE
MONOCHROME

BEST OF FRIENDS

The yearbook of Creative Monochrome

Editor: ROGER MAILE ARPS

Published in the UK by Creative Monochrome Ltd
20 St Peters Road, Croydon, Surrey, CR0 1HD.

British Library Cataloguing-in-Publication Data:
A catalogue record for this book is available from the British Library

ISBN 1 873319 16 9
First edition, 1994

Printed in England by The Bath Press,
Lower Bristol Road, Bath, Avon.

Introduction

Roger Maile

Best of Friends is a selection from the work of around 1,700 photographers who had chosen to register as 'Friends of Creative Monochrome' by the end of May 1994.

In introducing this volume, I hope it will be helpful to describe what Creative Monochrome is and who its Friends are, and then to try to explain – rather than justify – the selection process.

Creative Monochrome

Firstly, I should introduce myself, because Creative Monochrome is my baby. I've been keen on photography since childhood, with a bias towards monochrome work, although not to the point of exclusivity. Through a number of career moves, directed more by chance than good planning, I have gained experience in writing, editing and publishing.

When, three years ago, I had to get used to starting my age with a '4' rather than a '3', it seemed like a good time to take stock of what I was doing and where I was going. Believing that life is not a rehearsal but the actual performance, and being all too conscious of how many opportunities had already been wasted, it seemed like a good time to seek a fresh direction.

'Mid-life crisis' may be the phrase which most commonly comes to mind, but I cannot honestly say it was anywhere near as traumatic as that suggests. I simply decided to use whatever talents or abilities I could muster to do something that I would enjoy and find fulfilling. That really did not represent any form of hardship. Whereas others in similar circumstances have discovered missions of great moral value for the good of humanity, my own solution was somewhat more mundane: to start a photographic publishing business. I chose to concentrate initially in monochrome, partly because I find it a more expressive medium, but also because the costs of colour printing are intimidating.

As the idea developed, however, it did begin to take on a sense of mission beyond the remit of a normal commercial enterprise. It became apparent at a very early stage that there was a great wealth of talented photographers who were being frustrated in their desire to share their work with a wider audience, whether through books, magazines or exhibitions. I initially believed that this was a particular UK problem, but now believe it is virtually universal.

A particularly perverse parallel to this problem, in my view, was the relatively abundant opportunities and public funding made available to support anything that masqueraded under the 'leading edge' banner, or whose perpetrators were deemed 'politically correct'. I know it seems bitter and twisted to lament 'positive discrimination' in favour of disabled black lesbians, but I gained the distinct impression that unless I found such authors or published work which no-one would want to look at (let alone buy), I would be actively discriminated against by the Arts Council and the rest of the arts 'mafia'.

In my opinion, a lot of the 'leading edge' work that gets an undue proportion of the attention, exhibition space and public funding is mediocre both in concept and technical execution. It reflects more the failure of aesthetic discrimination of a small band of 'gate-keepers', who are running scared of being condemned as passé or conservative in their selection. They view images as an intellectual exercise rather than an emotional and sensory experience. They share a perverse value system by which the positive standards, judgements and reactions that 'normal' mortals would apply to images count as negatives. Images which are normally regarded as pleasing and uplifting, technically excellent and skilfully executed in terms of composition, lighting, and printing, are non-starters.

That is not to say that I am a dyed-in-the-wool traditional pictorialist – well, not in my own opinion. I do accept the desirability of exploring the possibilities of this fascinating medium, of venturing into new areas, and of challenging established practices. What I cannot accept is the desire to throw the baby out with the exhausted developer.

So Creative Monochrome, as I called the publishing venture, presented the opportunity to redress the balance and give some of those photographers who had been overlooked the opportunity to share their work with a wider audience. To me, this is important, because I believe that any form of self-expression needs an audience to make it live. So many photographers have been condemned to sharing their images with just a narrow circle of friends or in club competitions and then packing them away in a premature graveyard of drawers and boxes. A rich heritage of photographic talent and art has suffered this living death.

Thus, the photographic books which Creative Monochrome has produced have been distinguished by the dominant influence of the image rather than text. One manifestation of this which I wish other publishers would copy is that the images are given room to breathe on the page and that no image ever crosses the spine of the book. The books are, in the main, very simple and straightforward presentations of the photographers' portfolios.

Friends of Creative Monochrome

As this sense of mission unfolded, and as I began to realise the extent of the commercial challenge I had undertaken, it became clear that I needed to encourage like-minded people to get behind the idea, providing support not just in terms of buying the books, but in evangelising for the cause and encouraging others to participate.

With this in mind, Friends of Creative Monochrome was formed in November 1992. By the end of the following year, membership exceeded 1,000 and this number had doubled eight months later, with Friends registered in over 30 countries outside the UK.

From the outset, I was determined that Friends would be different. There is no subscription or membership fee and no obligation to purchase, but Friends receive benefits such as a free quarterly newsletter, special offers, the chance to buy signed copies of books, prize draws of exhibition prints and so forth. The economic rationale is that books sold direct to Friends avoid discounts to bookshops and commission to salesmen and distributors, whilst building the mailing list meant that the people most likely to be interested in Creative Monochrome's titles would be well informed of what was available.

Friends of Creative Monochrome has surpassed even my ambitious hopes for it, not just in terms of numbers and sales of books, but in the support and enthusiasm which has been generated. So many have commented that this is exactly what they had been waiting for and have backed this with very practical and generous support. I wanted to encourage this active participation in the development of Creative Monochrome and *Best of Friends* emerged as one of the ways of achieving this.

Best of Friends

The idea behind *Best of Friends* was to give the opportunity of having images published to a much wider group than is possible through the normal sole author publishing route. There are not many photographers who can put together a coherent and consistently excellent portfolio of over 50 images, which is the usual starting point for a book. But many have individual photographs which really deserve to be seen. Thus, *Best of Friends* was conceived essentially as a published exhibition of the best work of members.

At the time that entries were first invited, there were around 1,500 Friends. Each Friend was entitled to submit up to 12 images. As my own target to monitor the success of the idea, I hoped to receive work from 150 photographers, expecting about 1,000 photographs in total. In the event, 242 photographers entered a total of 2,050 prints. I was as delighted with this response as I was daunted by the task of selection and administration. To do justice to the entry, I expanded the number of pages in the book, dropped the idea of including a full list of Friends (which would have occupied 9 pages), and severely curtailed the anticipated amount of supporting text.

From the outset, I had dismissed the idea of any form of selection committee. I could rationalise this in terms of wishing to avoid the compromises and complications that result from the exercise of democracy, but candidly it is as simple as not being willing to have others dictate to me what Creative Monochrome should publish. It also has the merit that you, the readers of this book, know who to blame if the selection shown does not meet with your approval!

It is traditional that any selector or judge says how difficult it was to make the final choice. I can only say that this was certainly true for *Best of Friends*. What I had planned to do in a couple of days, actually took the best part of a month – and, frankly, a very anguished month at that. Perhaps I should have expected this, as I was well aware that the Friends included many very accomplished workers.

I started with what I intended to be a very severe first round cull, which left me with just under 600 images to choose from. Frankly, this was not too difficult, because I could operate on the basis of 'when in doubt, leave it in'. My intention was that the next round would reduce the number of images to about 300. In fact, it took me two more complete runs to get the number down to 400, and even then I was leaving out images which I would certainly consider worthy of publication.

At this stage, I decided to sub-group the images into broadly themed sections, such as landscape, trees, water, figure, portraits and so forth. The sections were determined by the images I had selected rather than by selecting images to fit pre-determined themes. I felt it was appropriate that no individual section should be too dominant within the book, and this helped me to narrow down the numbers for the final selection. The final choice was very painful and partly determined by the need to create a natural flow through the book and between facing pages. Beyond the 161 images selected for the book, I kept back around 100 photographs which I believe should be published and which I hope to be able to use in future publications.

If that describes the process, what were the criteria I applied? In many respects, these were much the same as most club judges or exhibition selectors would use. I think the main respect in which selection for a book differs is the importance of the image being able to sustain interest. Competitions and exhibitions tend to place more emphasis on initial impact: the punch on the nose rather than the gentle but persuasive twist of the arm. An image in a book, however, has (if you will excuse the pun) a much longer shelf-life. It is important that a good proportion of the images are arm-twisters, repaying repeated viewing and prolonged contemplation by revealing new layers of meaning.

Any selection process for images, and that for this book is certainly no exception, is bound to be heavily dependent on the subjective prejudices and preferences of the selector. I am conscious that my selection will no doubt reveal the vast baggage of conscious and sub-conscious personal hang-ups which form as much a part of my being as anyone else's. And I'm sure that what I read into many of the photographs will differ widely from what others will see and feel.

What I can and do say, with great pleasure, is that there isn't a photograph in the book which I don't enjoy. And I hope that many readers will share that experience. Whether you do or not, I do urge you to take the trouble to express your views so that these can go into the melting pot which will emerge as *Best of Friends II*.

Index of contributors

(The index references are to image numbers, rather than page numbers)

Portfolio

1
Castlerigg Stones
Jim Shipp AFIAP

2 **Perched block – storm** *Tom Chatterley*

3 **Quadrilith** *Cliff Tweats*

4 **The King's Men** *Dudley Woods ARPS*

5 **Dawn at Castlerigg** *Dudley Woods ARPS*

6 **Dry river bed stones** *Roger Crane*

7 **Rock Patterns I** *Anne Newell LRPS*

8
Forms in rock
Rob Gray

9

Earth and sky

Michael Maguire FIPF ARPS

10
Cleavage
Joe Tymkow LRPS

11
The nature of wood
Jim Shipp

12
Ray Spence

13
Ciboletta Mesa, near Acoma, New Mexico, 1991
George E Todd

14
Pot, Tumacacori Mission, Arizona, 1991
George E Todd

15
Pioneer House, White Oaks, New Mexico, 1991
George E Todd

16
Works entrance, Jura, France, 1993
George E Todd

17 **Boney** *David G Wilding LRPS*

18 **National Health** *Bill Carden FRPS*

19 **All talk** *Tim West*

20 **Three women, Ireland** *Nick Warwick*

21
Looking back
H F (Aitch) Keeling

22
Passage, India
Linda Griffiths

23
Jungle cook
Derrick Furlong

24
Street kid, Karnak
Darren J Lay

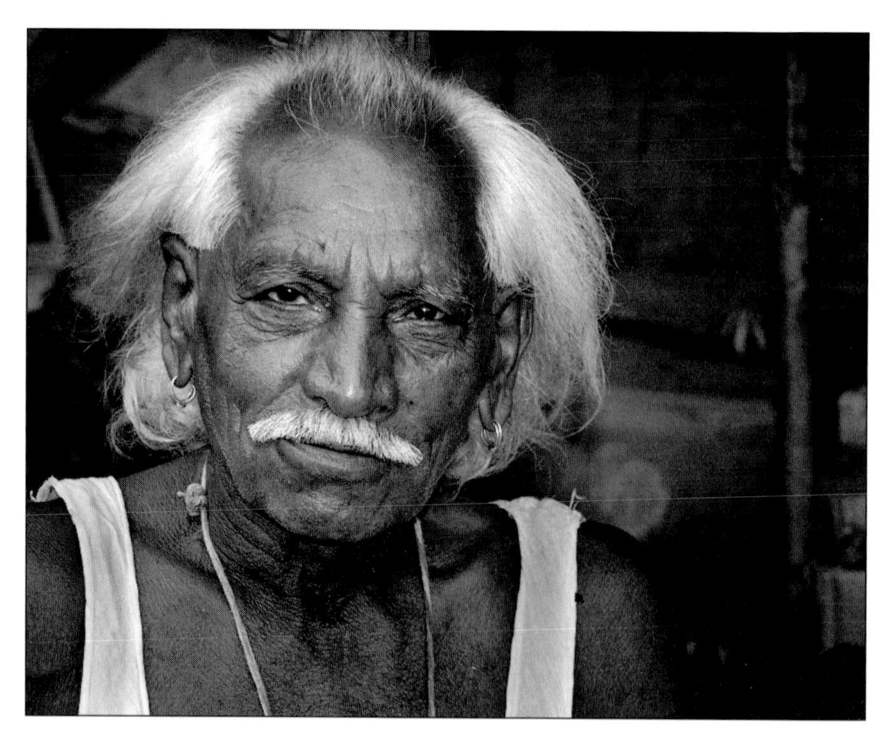

25 **Street trader, Delhi** *John Lloyd*

26 **Proud of his past** *Harry Weekers*

27 **Indian portrait** *Harry Weekers*

28 **Old gentleman** *James Dunn*

29
Interior
Jakab Tibor

30
Hotel du Commerce, Jura, France, 1993
George E Todd

31 **L'Albero II** *John Nasey FRPS*

32 **Poles apart** *John Nasey FRPS*

33
Belvedere I
John Nasey FRPS

34
Early morning, Lindisfarne
Trevor J Ingram ARPS

35
Sheep
David Swailes

36
Farmhouse
Patrick Reilly

37
Ovington Mill
John J Philpott MBE FRPS

38
Dawn, Ornockenock
Tom Richardson

39
The gate
Tom Richardson

40 **Frosty morning, Ashton Keynes** *Brian C Walker*

41 **Windswept** *David Pearce*

42 **River Talisker, Skye** *Trevor Crone*

43 **Grasses** *Peter Clark* FRPS AFIAP

44
Hedge and fence, Edale
Hugh Milsom

45
Bewick Hill
Peter Dixon

46
Dunes
David Hall

47
Desolate hut
Chris Shore FRPS

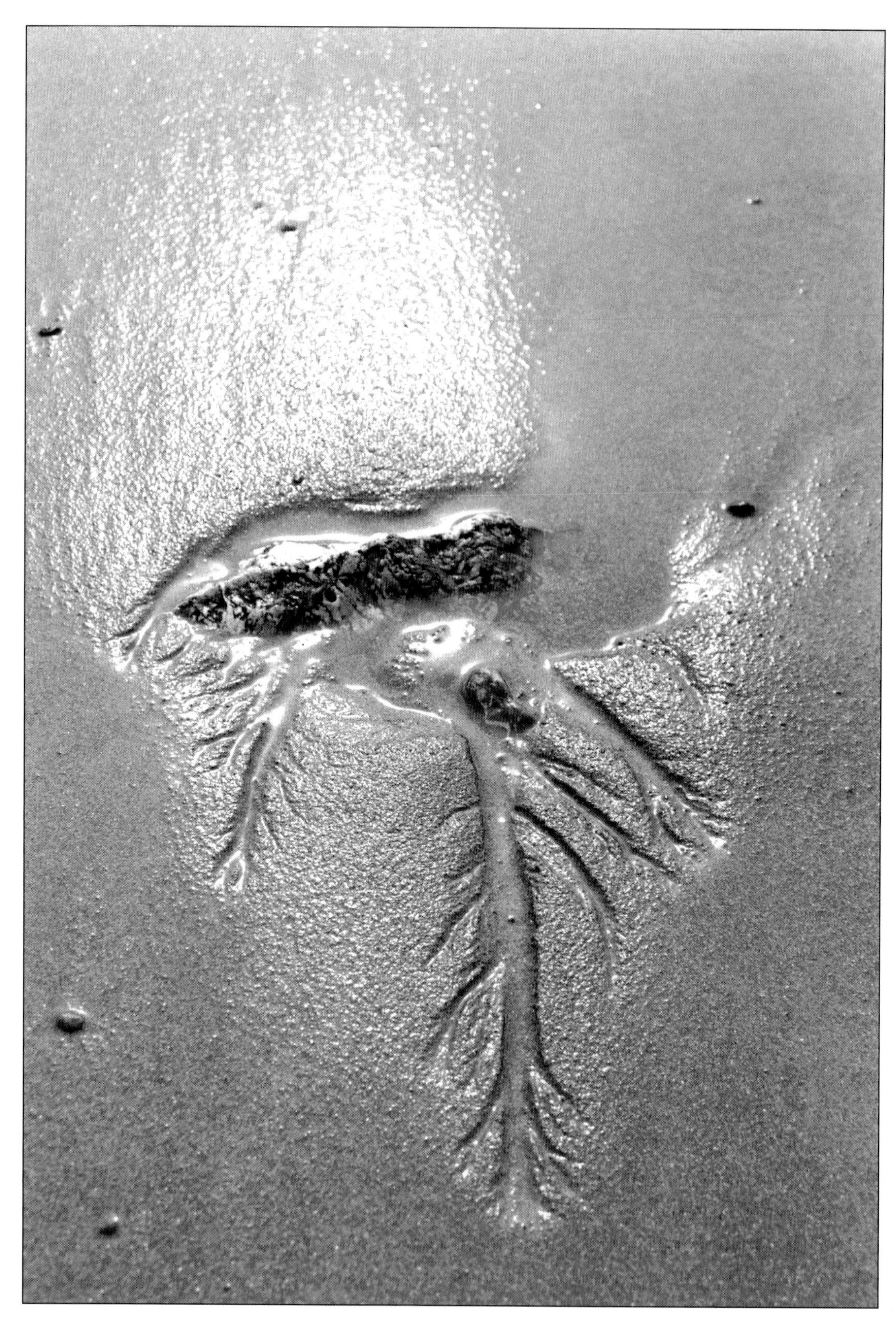

48
Beach patterns
Bill Rowntree ARPS

49

Fern frond

Vivienne M Smith LRPS

50
Mussel beds, Brittany
Philip Warren

51 **Winter field** *Richard Clegg*

52 **Sand dunes, Death Valley** *Leigh Preston*

53
Pavement pattern
David Hall

54
Creepers III
John Nasey FRPS

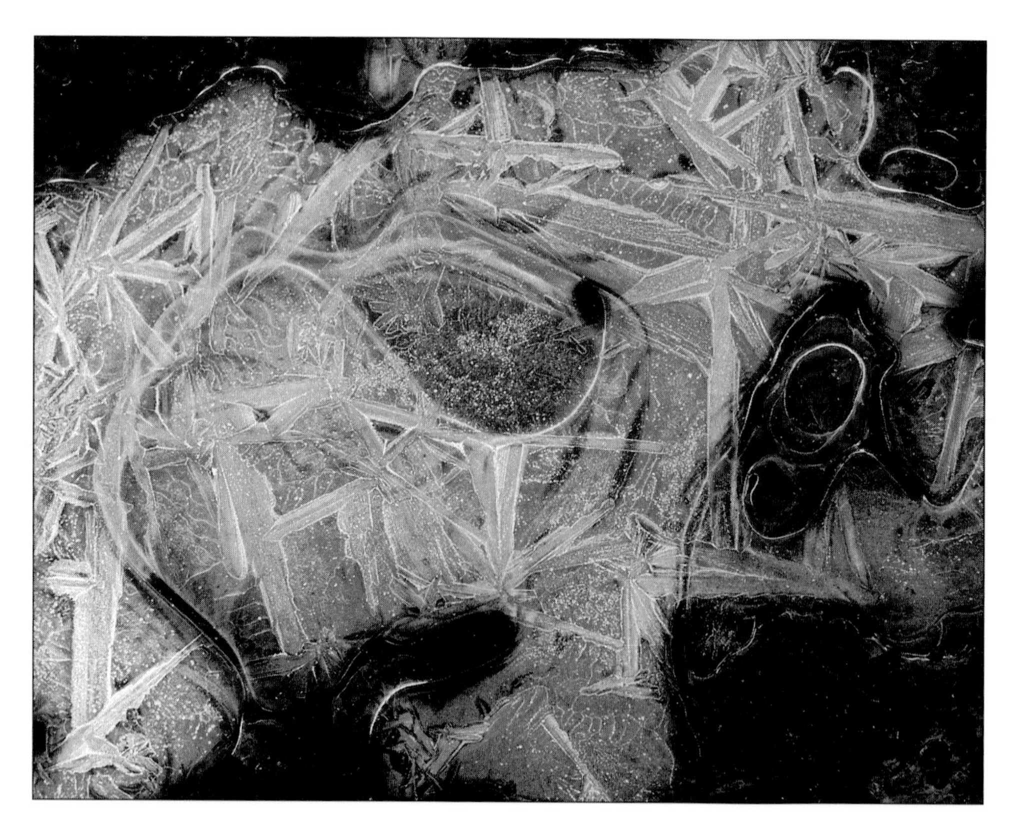

55 **Freeze** *Gary S Freeman*

56 **Black ice** *Mike Chambers* ARPS

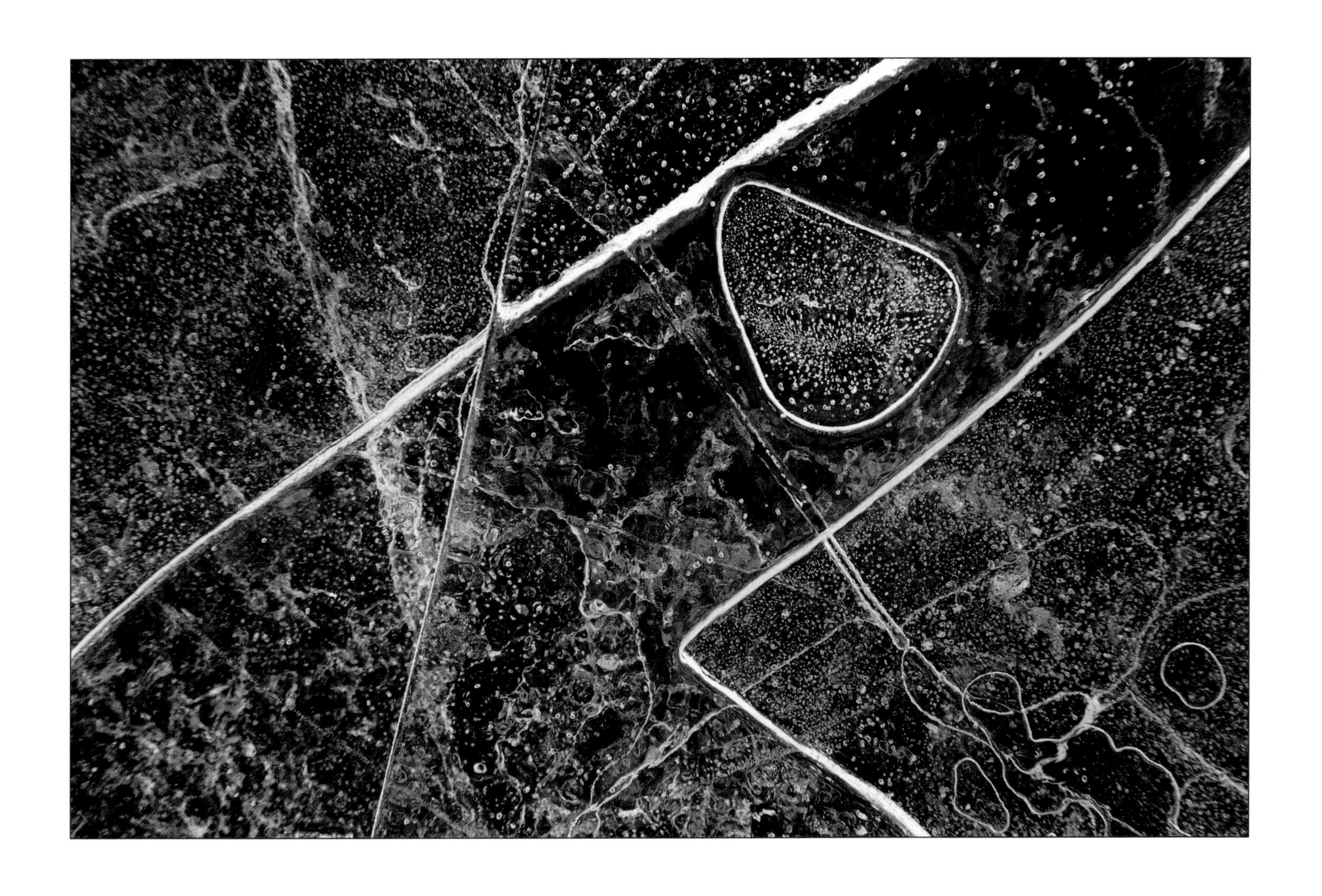

57
Ice angles
John Devenport ARPS

58
Water reflections
Sandy Wilson

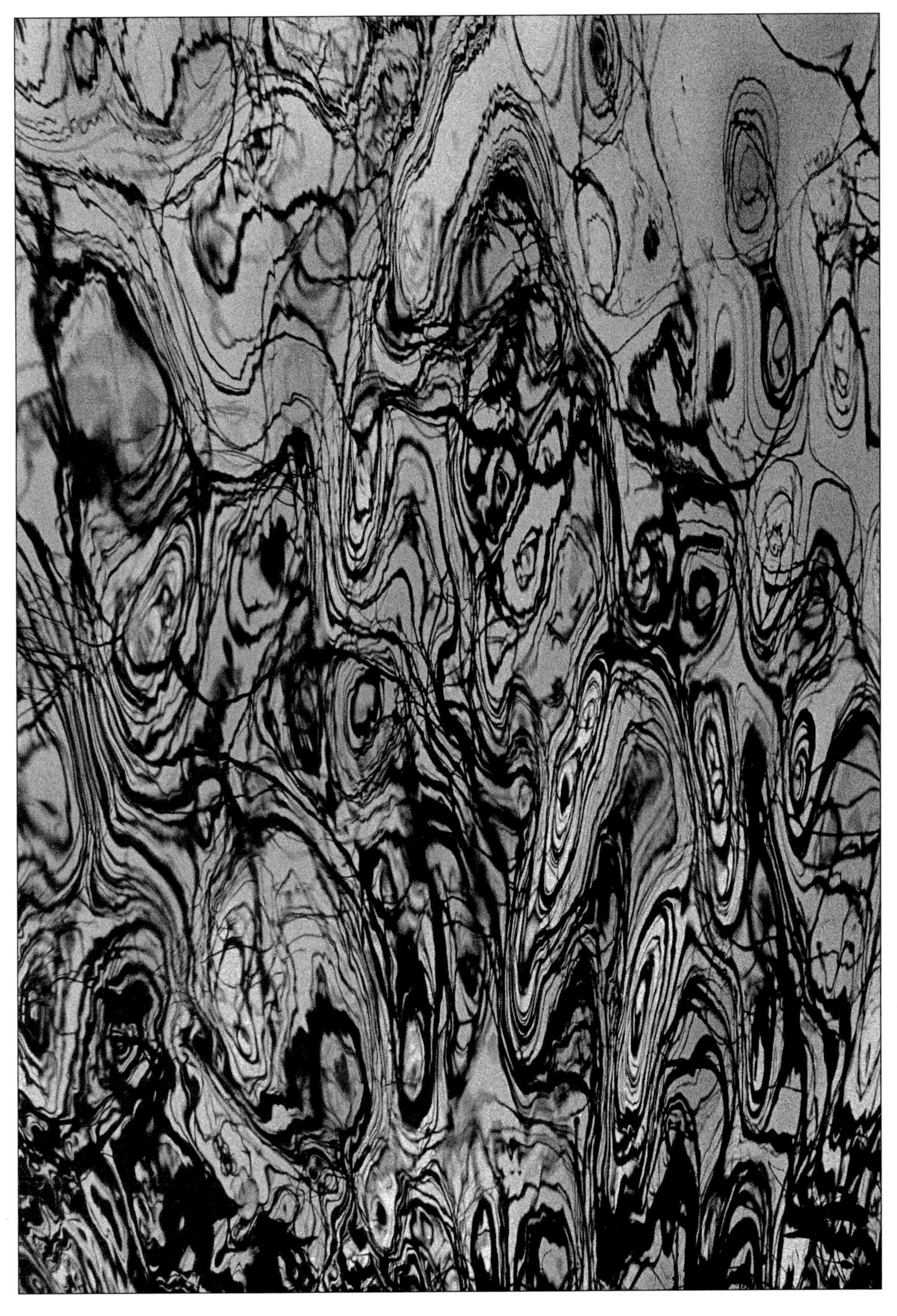

59
Reflections in the Thames, near Hampton Court
Jenifer Roberts

60 **Spiral** *Mary Davis*

61 **Garden steps, Heveningham Hall, Suffolk** *David Thorne*

62 **Station roof** *Gary S Freeman*

63 **Floor design, St Pauls Cathedral** *Sandy Wilson*

64 **Descent**

65 **Diagonal layout**

64-67
La Défense, Paris
Rosalind Bramley ARPS

66 **Ascent I**

67 **Litter free**

68
Trinity
Hazel Sanderson ARPS

69
Candle smoke
Andrew Chapman

70
Harvest festival
Sue Davies ARPS

71
After the dust has settled
Alan Fowler ARPS

72
Watermark, near Cirencester
Brian C Walker

73
Floating
Andy Wilson

74
Paul Warner

75
Paul Warner

76 **Nude** *Barry Cook*

77 **Early one morning** *Peter Rees*

78 **Yevette #1** *Dave Miller*

79 **Reclining nude** *Roy Elwood*

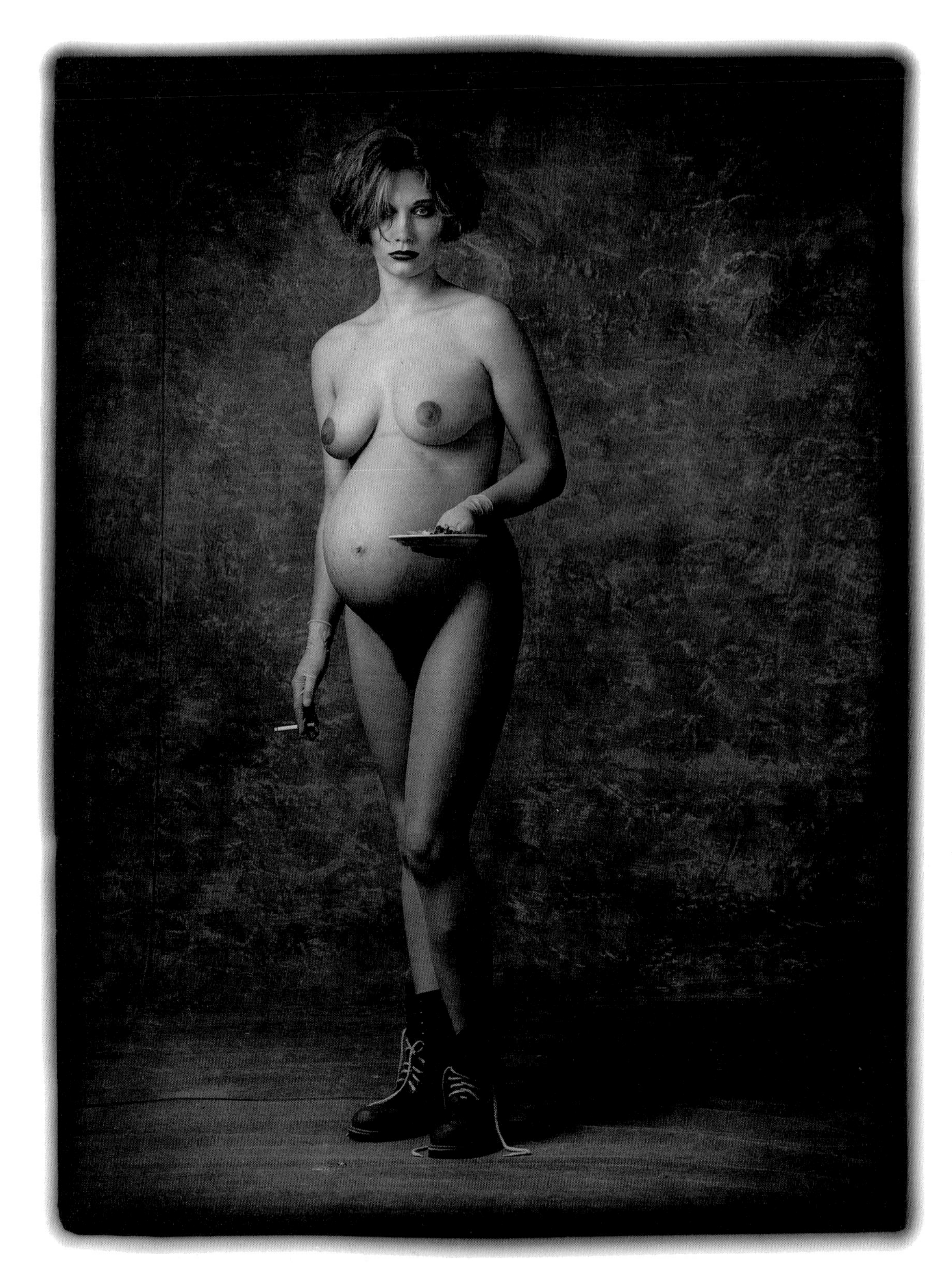

80
David Penprase

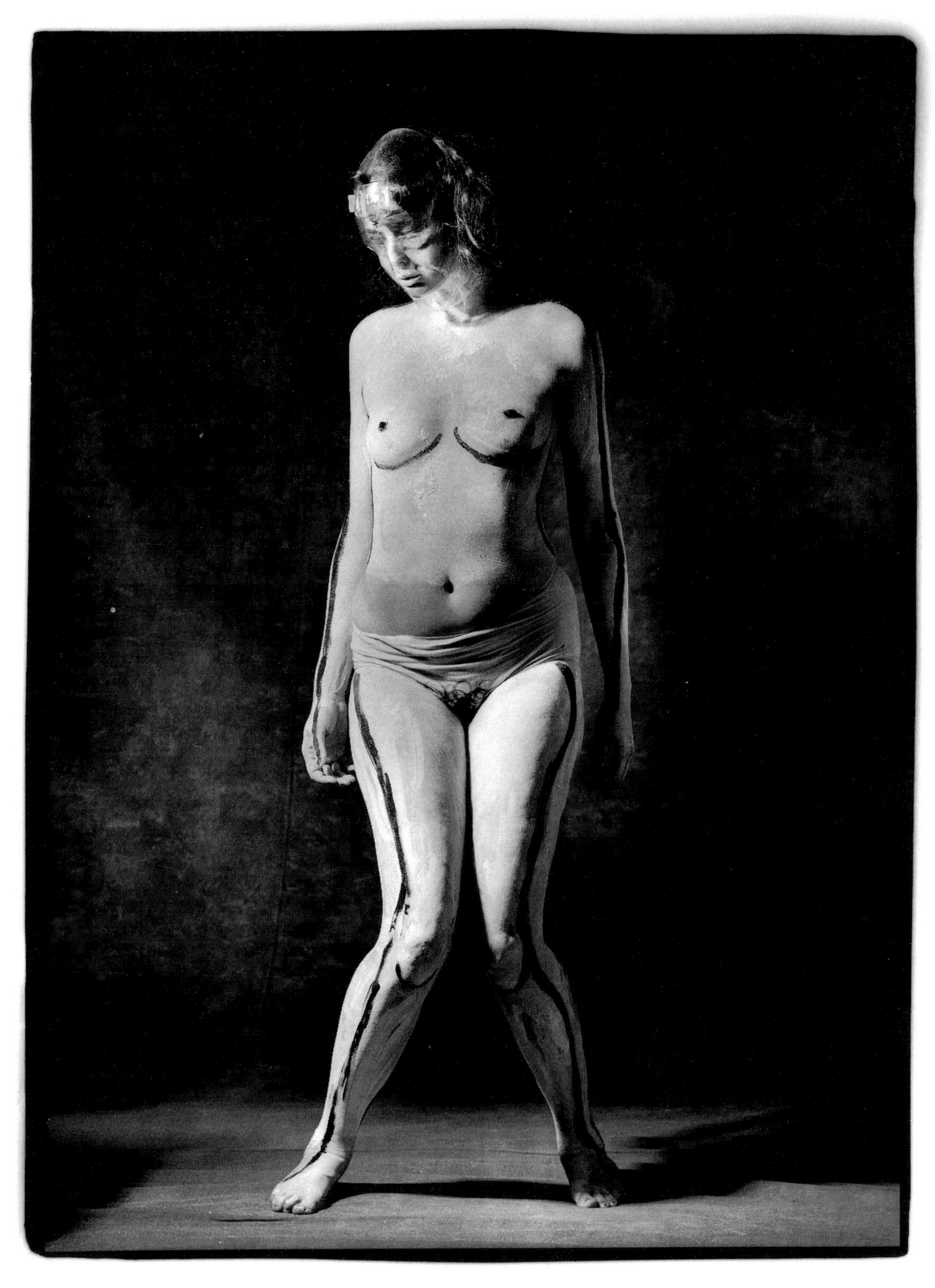

81
David Penprase

82 **Dawn mist** *Geoff Hodgson* ARPS

83 **Forest mist** *Dave Gordon* LRPS

84 **Foggy Chanctonbury** *Ken Wilson*

85 **At Gaddesden, November** *Richard Eldred*

86
Olive grove, Corfu
Philip Warren

87
Middle earth
Joe Tymkow LRPS

88 **The shining tree** *John Devenport* ARPS

89 **Surviving** *Arnold Hubbard*

90 **Spanish landscape** *Bill Wisden*

91 **Alpine storm** *David Oldfield*

92
Laxton
Glyn Jones FRPS

93
Frosted birch
Chris O'Reilly

94
Slate fence, Cwm Orthin, 1978
Tom Dodd

95
Roman wall and tree
Alan Fowler ARPS

96
Icy trees
Jean Wheeler

97
Underworld
Vivienne M Smith LRPS

98

Shadows in Sun Collonade, Harrogate

Mary Plunkett FRPS

99

Skeletal gate

Hazel Sanderson ARPS

100
Radiator
Anthony Corkhill LRPS

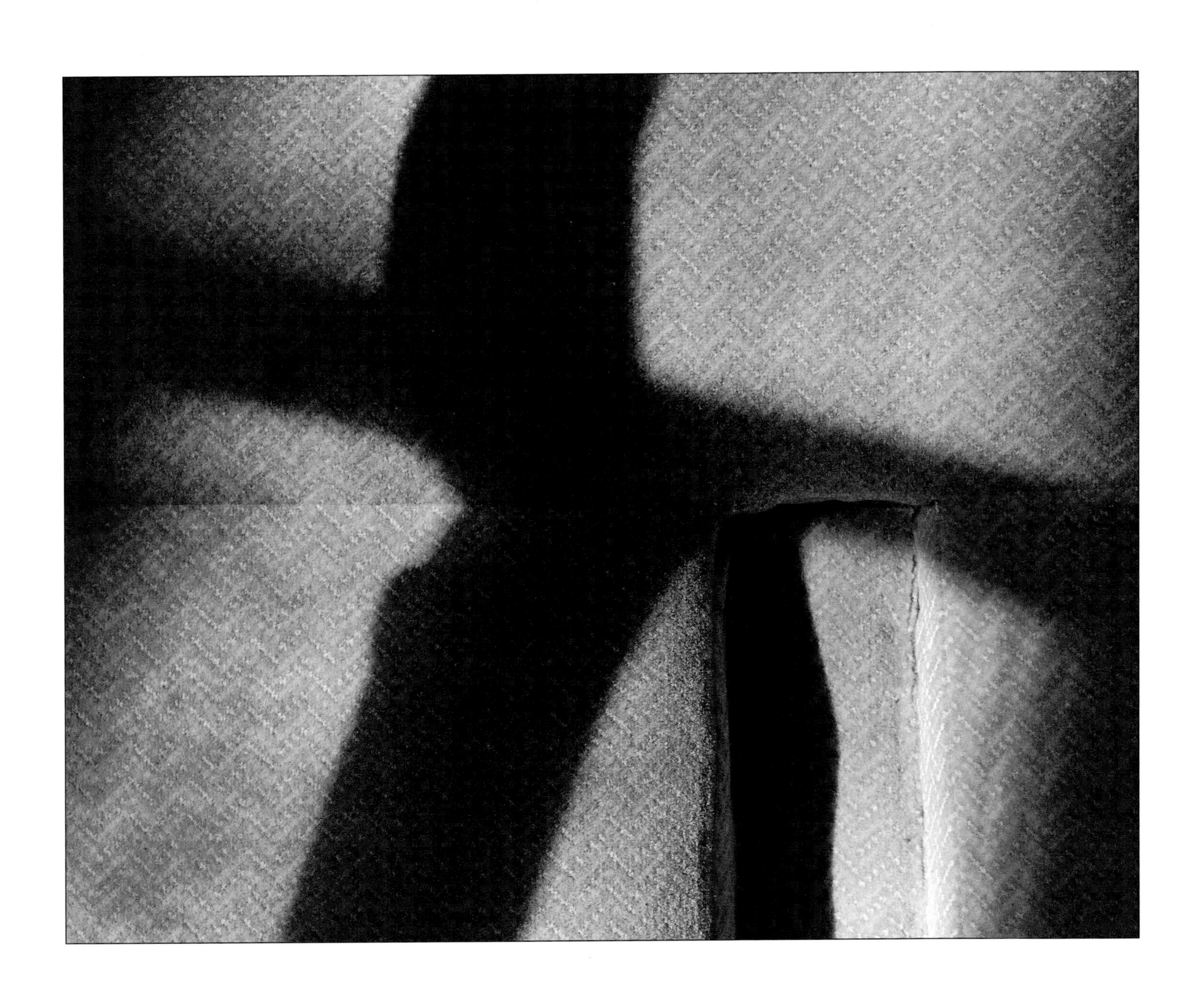

101
Seat with shadow
Anthony Corkhill LRPS

102
After the rain
Judith Lucas

103
Cobbles (after Brandt)
Andy Wilson

104
Demise
Peter Ruck LRPS

105
Old window detail
Frederick J Everett

106
Sunshine and showers
Ray Garcia

107
Monday, Monday
Margaret Rowntree

108
View from parents-in-law's house, Pontypridd
Darren Warner

109
End of the line
John Scarbro

110 **Black headed gull** *Tom Brydon*

111 **Cantering into the storm** *John J Philpott* MBE FRPS

112
Free flight
Roger Crane

113
Horse movement
Alan Fowler ARPS

114
Horseplay
Trevor J Ingram

115
At the sheep gathering
Mike Chambers

116
Cow on a foggy day
Colin Westgate

117
Cloche hat
Clive B Harrison FRPS

118
Sophie
Barry Cook

119
Pauline
Leigh Preston

120
Eleanor
Mike Healey

121
Darren
Roger Maile

122
Youth
Linda Griffiths

123
Bard
Clive B Harrison FRPS

124
Frank
Robert Hughes LRPS

125
Gerald the Clock
Preston Horspool

126
Confession
Peter Ruck LRPS

127 **Foot work** *John Schuler ARPS*

128 **Escalator, London Underground** *Jeremy Norgan*

129
Admiral's feathers
Alan Ainsworth

130
Filigree
Dave Gordon LRPS

131 **Cascade** *Dave Gordon LRPS*

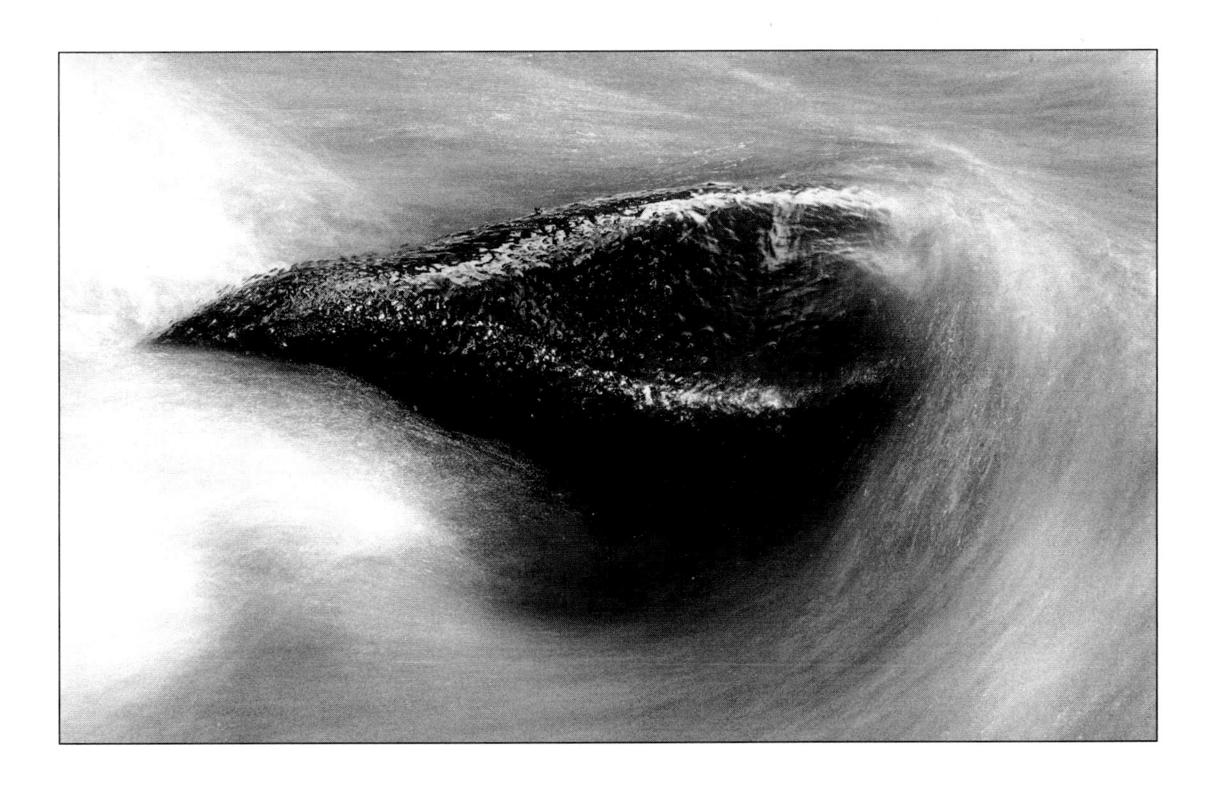

132 **Concorde** *Dave Gordon LRPS*

133
Snow and icicles
Len Perkis

134
Ice on rock
Len Perkis

135 **Time and tide** *Peter Clark FRPS, AFIAP*

136 **Tideflow** *Peter Clark FRPS, AFIAP*

137
Northumberland waterfall
Peter Dixon

138
From small beginnings
Preston Horspool

139

After the hail shower

Hazel Sanderson ARPS

140 **Frosting** *Alan Fowler* ARPS

141 **Winter leaves** *Anthony Corkhill* LRPS

142
Frozen web
John Rivoire

143 **Arum lily** *David Crawford*

144 **Ivy on prunus, Crathes Castle** *Jim Henderson* AMPA

145 **Apple** *Nancye Gault*

146 **Peace lily** *David Crawford*

147
Aftermath
Peter Millard

148
The ball boy
John Scarbro

149
Sinister window I
Trevor Crone

150
Sinister window II – the breakout
Trevor Crone

151
Paul Warner

152
A reverie
Gary S Freeman

153
Gazing
Chris O'Reilly

154
Memorial
Mark Snowdon

155 **Arts & craft sarcophagus, Brompton Cemetery, May 1993** *Aysen Slack*

156 **Sunlit steps, Venice** *M D Shorter*

157
Isadora Duncan, Pere Lachaise, September 1993
Aysen Slack

158 **Shoe Cove, Newfoundland, 1993** *George E Todd*

159 **Graveyard** *Patrick Reilly*

160 **Japanese tombstones** *Dr Chris Wainwright* FRPS

161 **In loving memory** *Colin Grinnell*

Contributor profiles

Those submitting work for this book were invited to supply a personal photographic profile. Available space has meant that these have had to be edited to a brief outline – with apologies for any vital information omitted or inaccuracies introduced! In a few cases, profiles were not provided and it proved impossible to get information prior to the print deadline. Where requested, photographic distinctions are shown alongside the photographer's name: others are referred to in the text. The italicised numbers in brackets at the end of each entry are the reference numbers of the images in the portfolio (ie not the page numbers). There is a glossary of abbreviations used in the profiles on page 144.

Alan Ainsworth *(Surrey)*
Alan has been a photographer for over 40 years, following in the footsteps of father and grandfather – the latter was wielding a plate camera before the first World War. Alan is a member of Reigate PS and is active as a speaker and judge in the Surrey Federation. His main interests are landscapes and candid photography of people. *(129)*

Rosalind Bramley ARPS *(Derbyshire)*
Rosalind has been interested in photography since childhood and is an enthusiastic member of North Cheshire PS and a committee member of the RPS North West region. She particularly enjoys producing monochrome 'geometrical' images. Rosalind has had one solo exhibition and several salon acceptances and competition successes. *(64-67)*

Tom Brydon *(Avon)*
Professionally, Tom has been doing commercial, industrial and architectural photography for some 25 years. He re-generates his photographic interest by combining his love of the British countryside with landscape photography. He especially likes taking his Leica M2 for walks in the hills and, of course, he only uses monochrome film. *(110)*

Bill Carden FRPS *(Buckinghamshire)*
Bill gained his RPS Fellowship in 1971 and was awarded the rare honour of a one-man exhibition in the Members' Gallery at the Octagon in 1993. He is a member of High Wycombe CC and the London Salon and serves on the RPS Pictorial distinctions panels. He is best known for his candid photography of people. *(18)*

Mike Chambers ARPS *(Surrey)*
Mike became seriously interested in photography about 12 years ago on joining Selsdon CC, drawing inspiration from the club's experienced workers. His many exhibition and competition successes indicate the efficacy of this route. Mike's main interests are in landscape and the shapes and textures of nature. *(56, 115)*

Andrew Chapman *(South Yorkshire)*
Over the last decade, Andrew's enthusiasm for monochrome photography has developed into fanaticism. Using mainly 35mm equipment, Andrew enjoys subjects such as portraits, land/cityscapes and close-up work. He finds that the mood or light first attracts him to his subject matter. Andrew has had several images published in books and magazines and accepted for exhibitions. *(69)*

Tom Chatterley *(Leicestershire)*
Tom's interest in photography dates back to the early 1960s, soon after he started work. An active mountaineer, landscape and mountain photography are his favourite subjects, although his membership of Earl Shilton CC has enouraged a very varied photographic diet. For monochrome work, Tom prefers to use medium format. *(2)*

Peter J Clark FRPS AFIAP *(Staffordshire)*
Peter has been a member of Cannock PS for over 15 years and is a well known judge and lecturer on the Midlands club circuit. He achieved his RPS distinctions for his monochrome landscape work. A prolific exhibitor in national and international exhibitions, Peter has over 600 acceptances to his name, including over 90 awards and 5 FIAP/PSA gold medals. *(43, 135, 136)*

Richard Clegg *(Worcestershire)*
Like so many other contributors, Richard's photographic enthusiasm developed as a result of joining a good camera club and learning from other members. Although he travels widely as part of his job, he finds that his best pictures are usually taken within five miles of his home. Richard gained his LRPS in 1993 and has had work accepted in national and international exhibitions. *(51)*

Barry Cook *(Surrey)*
Barry learned his photography the hard way – through a 13 year stint starting as a photographer's assistant, and his print quality to this day bears testimony to the value of such a training. His recent project, *Echoes have Eyes*, accompanied by the poetry of Liz Randell, has received an enthusiastic response as an exhibition and is being published as a book (under the same title) by Creative Monochrome. *(76, 118)*

Anthony Corkhill LRPS *(West Midlands)*
Having started at age 10, Anthony's enthusiasm for photography waned during the period he was building his career and business, to be rekindled around 1990. He gained his LRPS in 1993. Anthony works mainly in medium format and monochrome, doing all his own developing and printing, but confesses to the occasional use of a colour slide film. *(100, 101, 141)*

Roger Crane *(Kent)*
Roger has been taking photographs for over 35 years and is particularly interested in landscape work and the use of early photographic processes. As well as judging on the local club circuit, he has written several topic sheets for his local camera club. He is a Licentiate of the RPS and a member of the London Salon. *(6, 112)*

David Crawford *(London)*
David works in black and white and colour, taking "anything that interests me". He has been interested in photography for 15 years, during which time he gained an A-level in photography, studied graphic design and photography at art college, and finally took BA and MA degrees in graphic design at Leicester Polytechnic. Currently, he works as a freelance graphic designer and photographer. *(143, 146)*

Trevor Crone *(London)*
Having become interested in photography in 1973, Trevor has progressed to have work published in magazines and books, and as postcards and greetings cards (including 'Ice Ghost' for Creative Monochrome). He has exhibited widely and has won several national photographic competitions. He is the competition secretary for Greenwich PS. *(42, 149, 150)*

Sue Davies ARPS *(Buckinghamshire)*
Sue became hooked on photography as a result of enrolling on a City & Guilds modular photography course. Encouraged to visit galleries and exhibitions, she was particularly impressed by John Blakemore's Inscape exhibition and freely admits the obvious influence on her own work. Sue enjoys all forms of photography, but wherever she wanders, she always seems to return to still life picture-making. *(70)*

Mary Davis *(London)*
Mary has sustained a serious interest in photography for several years, juggling this with family commitments and a part-time job. She is currently working towards her LRPS through the City & Guilds scheme and is also taking an extra-mural photography course at the University of Hertfordshire. Her favourite subjects are still life, close-up and landscapes. *(60)*

John Devenport ARPS *(London)*
John has been making monochrome images for about 15 years and is an active member of Beckenham PS and the Mirage Group. He enjoys capturing the beauty and drama of the landscape, particularly in wilderness areas, and searching out bold, graphic images from both man-made and natural subjects. He gained his ARPS in 1988 with a panel of pictorial landscapes. *(57, 105)*

Peter Dixon *(Tyne & Wear)*
Peter has been interested in photography for over 30 years and is a member of Tyneside CC and Whickham CC. He gives talks on his monochrome prints to clubs in the Northern Counties Photographic Federation. With five other North East photographers, Peter formed the Imprint Group, whose aim is to promote photography through exhibitions around the North East. *(45, 137)*

Tom Dodd *(Gwynedd)*
Tom's photographic interest spans some 24 years, during most of which time it has been inseparable from his involvement with climbing and the outdoor environment. A well known lecturer, exhibitor and judge, Tom gained his FRPS in 1979 with a panel of monochrome mountain landscapes. He is a member of the London Salon and the licentiateship panel of the RPS. *(94)*

James Dunn *(Falkirk)*
Having worked in engineering after leaving school, James studied photography for two years in the early 1980s, before starting work for Glasgow Museums. He's still there and says he has "no real plans, unless Littlewoods or National Geographic get in touch"! *(28)*

Richard Eldred *(Hertfordshire)*
Richard's one-man exhibition, Gardens and Landscape, has been shown in Leicester and Derby, and he has also participated in several group exhibitions. His images have been published in several magazines and he is now developing a book of photographs of formal English gardens. *(225)*

Roy Elwood *(Tyne & Wear)*
Much of Roy's life centres around photography, especially monochrome – an enduring first love. He has shifted in recent years away from individual images towards sets of prints on themes, such as water, nudes and dancers. He is an Associate of the RPS, currently working towards the Fellowship distinction. *(79)*

Frederick J Everett *(Essex)*
Although starting to take photographs at the age of 13, it was not for a further 20 years until it became a real passion, when starting to print his own work. He is a member of Loughton CC. He describes his favourite subject matter currently as "life as it passes by". *(105)*

Alan Fowler ARPS *(Tyne & Wear)*
Alan is a member of Gateshead CC and gained his Associateship of the RPS in 1989. He describes his main interest in photography as "capturing light, mood and feeling within the print. To me, the subject matter is not that important – it is the combination of these ingredients, in my opinion, which makes the image successful and lasting". *(71, 95, 113, 140)*

Gary S Freeman *(North Yorkshire)*
Having been taking photographs for about 10 years, Gary describes photography as a passion, and a photograph as "life holding its breath". A fan of Sylvia Plachy, he says he can't better her comment: "everywhere I go I carry these weights, my cameras. Maybe I'd float without these anchors". *(55, 62, 152)*

Derrick Furlong *(Lincolnshire)*
Derrick spent over 10 years living in Peru, earning a living from his still and cine photography, and working as a 'stringer' for news agencies. Living back in the UK since 1978 and still working as a press photographer, Derrick also organises ecology tours to South America. His preferred subject in monochrome photography is people in their environment. *(23)*

Ray Garcia *(Kent)*
Ray became seriously interested in photography over 40 years ago. Photography goes hand-in-hand with his other main source of enjoyment – walking on the fells and among the mountains, both in the UK and overseas. Although landscapes feature in Ray's work, he keeps his eyes open for any other subject with interesting lighting and patterns. *(106)*

Nancye Gault *(London)*
Nancye says that she really got going on the making of photographs when she started a City & Guilds course at Richmond Adult Centre, which led on to a BTEC National Diploma and the award of her LRPS. In her work as a nurse in a maternity unit, she enjoys recording the rapport between new babies, their mothers and the people who work with them. *(145)*

Dave Gordon LRPS *(Devon)*
A recently retired fireman, Dave's interest in photography dates back 15 years. He started doing his own printing after joining a local camera club. His main interest is in monochrome landscape work, and particularly stone and water. Dave's images have been published in the local press and photographic magazines and he has had work exhibited locally. *(83, 130-132)*

Rob Gray *(Australia)*
Rob's interest in photography stems from the apparently obligatory pilgrimage of young Australians to Europe on leaving school. The photos became more important than the trip and he embarked on a career in photography. He abandoned this during the 1980s in favour of playing with computers, but has now adopted a 5x4 field camera to pursue his 'contemplative fine art photography'. *(8)*

Linda Griffiths *(East Sussex)*
Linda has become hooked on monochrome after four years of processing and printing. She likes to have total control from seeing the image to making and toning the fibre-based print. Like many other contributors, she felt a little restricted for this book having to limit her prints to 10x8" on resin-coated paper, untoned. Her main interest at the moment is photographing people, but she hopes to find time to try some landscape work in future. *(22, 94)*

Colin Grinnell *(Worcestershire)*
Colin took O- and A-level photography at West Bromwich College of Art and Design, before moving to Worcestershire, where he taught photography part-time at Evesham College of Further Education. In 1985, he had a panel of 12 prints shown in the Young Photographers series at Lacock Abbey. His favourite camera is a "beat-up old Rolleicord which cost £30". *(161)*

David Hall *(Tyne & Wear)*
David's photographic enthusiasm was kindled in 1983 on joining Gateshead Camera Club, where he is currently President. He gained his Associateship of the RPS in 1993 in pictorial monochrome and has recently been awarded the BPE1. David is a founder member of a small independent group, Imprint. *(46, 53)*

Clive B Harrison FRPS *(Berkshire)*
Clive is a member of the London Salon and of the widely acclaimed Arena Group and was a long-serving member of the RPS Licentiateship admissions panel. A regular exhibitor and award winner, his images have graced many magazines and books. His book of child photography, *Age of Innocence*, was published by Creative Monochrome in 1994. *(117, 123)*

Mike Healey *(Surrey)*
Mike specialises in the photography of people and his work has won him two portrait competitions in the Central Association and acceptances in various exhibitions, including the London Salon. He is a committee member of both Selsdon CC and The Camera Club. *(120)*

Jim Henderson AMPA *(Grampian)*
Jim became a full-time professional in 1986, specialising in work for the tourist-related industries through his BAPLA photo-library. He is the author of one of the Photographers' Britain titles and has had a solo exhibition in Aberdeen. *(8)*

Geoff Hodgson ARPS *(Worcestershire)*
Geoff has been interested in all aspects of photography for some 25 years. He is currently working almost exclusively in monochrome and concentrating on the impact of the smaller fine print. His main interest lies in the pictorial type of image, where a strong sense of form, pattern, texture and, of course, lighting, provide the essential ingredients for fine prints. *(82)*

Preston Horspool *(Essex)*
Since seeing his father-in-law working in the darkroom eight years ago, photography has become Preston's main hobby. He believes people regard him as slightly eccentric because of the depth of his involvement with art and photography. His main interests in photography are portraits and landscapes, normally using a Hasselblad and printing with a cold cathode enlarger. *(125, 138)*

Arnold Hubbard *(Tyne & Wear)*
Arnold has been a member of Sunderland PA for almost 25 years. Best known for his winter photography of the North East Dales and for his infra-red work, Arnold's work has been seen in many national and international exhibitions. A Fellow of the RPS and holder of the EFIAP distinction, Arnold is a popular lecturer and regular judge on the club circuit. *(89)*

Robert Hughes LRPS *(Gwent)*
Robert's interest in photography became serious in the early 1980s. He has concentrated particularly on landscapes and people as his subjects. A member of the Leica and RPS Pictorial Group postal portfolios, he has also gained some acceptances in national exhibitions. He is now working on an Associateship pictorial panel. *(124)*

Trevor J Ingram ARPS *(Herefordshire)*
Trevor describes himself as "a retiree who aspires to being a black and white art photographer". Although he sees himself as a generalist with a mainly traditional approach, he tries to fully exploit modern materials, equipment and art forms, including those outside the photographic. He is an active participant in club activities, societies and specialist small groups. *(34, 170)*

Jakab Tibor AFIAP (Romania)
Tibor works as a mechanical engineer, but as he says, "photography is what I really like to do". In the absence of photographic courses in Romania, he has learnt photography from books. He has staged several personal exhibitions in Romania, Hungary and England, and has had numerous acceptances in international and national salons, gaining the distinctions of AFIAP and one-star exhibitor of the PSA. *(29)*

Glyn Jones FRPS *(Nottinghamshire)*
Glyn started taking photographs while in primary school, which he reckons to be exactly 50 years ago. He has a particular interest in archaeology and landscapes, especially in Wales. He is secretary of Newark PS and is on the local Federation judges list. *(92)*

H F (Aitch) Keeling *(West Midlands)*
Starting his hobby in 1981, Aitch was soon instrumental in forming Wallheath CC, where he is currently programme secretary. He is also a member of Smethwick PS and an Associate of the RPS. Aitch exhibits locally, nationally and internationally, picking up a number of awards and competition successes. *(21)*

Darren J Lay *(Surrey)*
Discontent with his 'happy snapshots', Darren bought a cheap slr and studied successfully for O- and A- level photography, followed by a BTEC National Diploma. He is currently assisting an advertising photographer in London, but likes to indulge his passion for photo-journalism in foreign climes whenever he gets the opportunity. *(24)*

John Lloyd *(Lancashire)*
John describes himself as an average club member, starting comparatively late in life and "only having been involved for sixteen years". He has acceptances at national and international level, mainly for his colour printing from negatives. He now spends too much time in photographic administration at area and national level, being the Distinction Secretary for the newly instituted PAGB Awards for Photographic Merit. *(25)*

Judith Lucas *(West Midlands)*
Having gained her LRPS for colour slides, Judith's club – Wythall PS – persuaded her to try monochrome printing. Although intending to progress to colour once she had mastered the basics, she became hooked on monochrome and has already had exhibition acceptances. "I am still very much a learner, who is only just starting to 'see' in black and white." *(102)*

Michael Maguire FIPF ARPS *(Northern Ireland)*
Monochrome landscapes are Michael's main interest. He has had his work printed in many photographic magazines and accepted annually for exhibitions. He has been awarded top print in the PAGB exhibition and is on the international judging list. He states, simply, "I enjoy my photography". *(9)*

Roger Maile *(Surrey)*
Roger runs Creative Monochrome and consequently has depressingly little time to pursue his own photographic interests. He particularly enjoys photographing people and has published a behind-the-scenes book on Trinity Boys Choir, *A Choir for all Seasons*. He is an Associate of the RPS, a member of Selsdon CC and often judges and lectures on the local camera club circuit. *(121)*

Peter Millard *(Essex)*
Peter has been a keen amateur for over 30 years and is a member of two local camera clubs. He is a regular entrant of both national and international exhibitions, with what he describes as a "moderate success rate". He has just started work on producing "a talk or two to share with others my enthusiasm for the hobby". *(147)*

Dave Miller *(Tyne & Wear)*
Although he started taking photographs 20 years ago, it is only in the last 5 years that Dave has taken it more seriously. He has found his local camera club helpful in progressing his work, particularly in being able to see, show and discuss photographs. He is happy to tackle almost any subject, and has just mounted his first solo exhibition in a local library. *(78)*

Hugh Milsom *(Hertfordshire)*
Best known for his landscape photography, Hugh has been making photographs for over 30 years. Reflecting his many successes in national and international exhibitions, he has gained the MFIAP distinction. A member of Ware PS and Shillington CC, Hugh is currently preparing a book for publication by Creative Monochrome. *(44)*

John Nasey FRPS *(Channel Islands)*
Although only taking up photography some 10 years ago, John has already progressed to Fellowship of the RPS and has been entering national and international exhibitions since 1988. Since the following year, he has been teaching monochrome photography courses at the Jersey Art Centre. *(31-33, 54)*

Anne Newell LRPS *(Cornwall)*
Anne took up photography some 25 years ago, but after a prolonged period of abstinence from the hobby, took it up again a few years ago with renewed vigour. One fruit of this enthusiasm was the gaining in 1993 of her Licentiateship of the RPS. A member of a small, but friendly and enthusiastic, camera club, Anne's main interest is in landscape photography. *(7)*

Jeremy Norgan *(West Yorkshire)*
To quote: "My dad taught me to develop films and the basics of printing when I was ten, but I didn't really take up photography until I graduated in 1982. My interests are mostly in the general area of landscape photography, both rural and urban, though I make the occasional attempt at documentary photography. That's it!" *(128)*

David Oldfield *(Australia)*
David started taking photographs as a schoolboy in Huddersfield, before moving in 1967 to Australia. His main interest is combining monochrome landscape photography with bushwalking in the Victorian Alps. David is the junior vice-president of the Australian Photographic Society and a well known international exhibitor. *(91)*

Chris O'Reilly *(Derbyshire)*
Chris's interest in photography stemmed from a desire to photograph the pop groups of his youth. Since enrolling for a part-time A-level photography course in 1990, Chris has become interested in monochrome photographic art. However, his main interest is in the field of natural history photography, and Chris is currently studying for a degree in Biological Imaging at the University of Derby. *(93, 153)*

David Pearce *(Hertfordshire)*
David started making photographs at the age of 11, using a home-made, wooden contraption as an enlarger. Still preferring monochrome, he enjoys candid photography as well as pictorial. Some of his prints have been accepted for major exhibitions, but he is not very active in this field: "I tend to take pictures to please myself: if others appreciate them, then this is a welcome bonus." *(41)*

David Penprase *(Cornwall)*
David is a dedicated photographer whose work has been widely exhibited and has gained numerous awards in national and international exhibitions. He is a popular lecturer on photography and workshop tutor. Creative Monochrome published a portfolio of David's work in 1994, under the apt title, *Untitled*: David prefers to let his images talk directly to the viewer. *(80, 81)*

Len Perkis *(Norway)*
Since taking early retirement five years ago, Len has devoted most of his time to making photographs. His main subject interests are landscape, nature and travel. Len has had images published in many prestigious books and magazines and a major shipping line has used many of his landscapes to decorate its ships. He has been invited to exhibit in the United States this year. *(133, 134)*

John J Philpott MBE FRPS *(Hampshire)*
John was awarded the MBE for his services to the Ordnance Survey, where he was official photographer for 10 years. John is a well known lecturer in local photographic clubs and his work is frequently represented in national and international exhibitions. He specialises in photographing people and his book, *Face the Camera*, was published by Creative Monochrome in 1994. *(37, 111)*

Mary Plunkett FRPS *(West Sussex)*
Mary took up photography 14 years ago and is still using the same type of camera – Pentax ME – as when she started. She includes among her preferred subjects: still life, botanical, environmental portraiture, modern

architecture, mediaeval churches, landscapes and townscapes. Mary's chief photographic aim now is to have some of her work published. *(98)*

Leigh Preston *(Gloucestershire)*
Leigh's work has appeared in numerous magazines and exhibitions. A Fellow of the RPS, Leigh lectures widely on photography and is a member of the RPS licentiate distinctions panel. His main area of interest is pictorial photography. His portfolio of images on the disappearing industrial landscape was published as *Shadows of Change* by Creative Monochrome in 1993. *(52, 119)*

Peter Rees *(Shropshire)*
(77)

Patrick Reilly *(Eire)*
Patrick has been taking photographs since the 1970s, and enjoys a wide variety of aspects of the hobby, although still finding monochrome the most exciting medium. He writes, "While I think about my work, I don't feel the need to explain it in detail: if other people like it, I see that as a bonus." *(36, 159)*

Tom Richardson *(Lancashire)*
Tom has been interested in photography for 20 years, and has been taking it seriously for the last 8. An Associate of the RPS and holder of the BPE(2 star) distinction, Tom's work has been accepted by a number of salons and national exhibitions. He was a finalist in the 1993 Durst Master Printer competition. Tom's preferred subject is landscape and his ambition is to publish a book. *(38, 39)*

John Rivoire *(Essex)*
John has been creating monochrome images for around seven years. He is a member of Woodford PS and won the monochrome section in the Redbridge Arts Council photographic competition in 1992. In 1994, his employer used four of John's images in its calendar. He is currently preparing an Associateship panel for the RPS. *(142)*

Jenifer Roberts *(Surrey)*
A Fellow of the RPS, Jenifer exhibits regularly. She taught photography in adult education for several years and gives workshops on landscape photography and monochrome printing. She works only in monochrome, placing great emphasis on meticulous printing. A book of her photographs, *Spirit of the Place*, was published by Creative Monochrome in 1992. *(59)*

Bill Rowntree ARPS *(Gwynedd)*
Having been both a professional scientific photographer and an enthusiastic amateur for 40 years, Bill has just taken early retirement to become purely amateur. He writes, "Monochrome has been my first and last love, discarding the undesirable reality of colour. Form, texture and a sense of inevitability are important to me in my photography." *(48)*

Margaret Rowntree *(Gwynedd)*
Margaret had been taking slides for around 25 years, until she decided about four years ago to try her hand at monochrome: "Under the expert tuition of my husband, I found that I really enjoyed printing, and haven't taken a slide since." Margaret has already had what she describes as a 'modicum' of success in competitions and magazine publications. *(107)*

Peter Ruck LRPS *(Avon)*
Peter has been making photographic images for many years and his main interest has always been monochrome, "a medium which I find gives more satisfaction and more scope to the imagination than the more factual world of colour". He is the programme secretary for North West Bristol CC and, since retiring 18 months ago, has recently gained his Licentiateship of the RPS. *(104, 126)*

Hazel Sanderson ARPS *(West Yorkshire)*
Hazel is best known for her landscape photography and, in particular, her evocative images of the Yorkshire Dales – she is currently preparing a portfolio of this work for publication by Creative Monochrome. She describes her photographs as "a simple statement of a sensitive awareness of the beauty of the natural world, combined with a sense of wonder and respect". *(68, 99, 139)*

John Scarbro *(Lincolnshire)*
Interested in monochrome photography for about seven years, John has a liking for grainy, high contrast prints. He is a member of a small exhibition group, the Drove Photographic Group, which has mounted several exhibitions in the UK. A five year project producing images of the Lincolnshire seaside has generated material for his Fellowship of the RPS and an exhibition in the Museum of Lincolnshire Life. *(109, 148)*

John Schuler ARPS *(Oxfordshire)*
John became seriously interested in photography soon after the war, and joined the Hampshire House CC, where he was inspired by the outstanding work of many senior members, for whom he still retains the highest respect. John has worked as a freelance photographer and graphic designer. His images have been exhibited locally and published in several magazines. *(127)*

Jim Shipp AFIAP *(Northumberland)*
Jim is a member (since 1977) and past President of Hexham and District PS. He didn't get round to monochrome work until 1986 and remains better recognised for his colour nature photography, which has gained many competition successes and exhibition acceptances. *(1, 11)*

Chris Shore FRPS *(Kent)*
Chris is a member of the Mirage group, Romney Marsh CC and Ashford CC, and is a Kent County senior judge. His great love is capturing the beauty of Romney Marsh, so much so that he prefers his location to be given as Dungeness rather than Kent, claiming that Romney Marsh is a continent in its own right: "when the mist has risen and combines with a good sunrise, it can be a wonderful combination. It is just good to be there!" *(47)*

M D Shorter *(Somerset)*
Mr Shorter's main interest in photography has been pictorial in nature, and he makes no apology if some of this has been 'chocolate box': "if studies of the beautiful scene give pleasure to the viewer, then I believe it serves a legitimate purpose". He has spent much time recently copying old photographs and has a particular interest in the early photographic processes. (156)

Aysen Slack *(London)*
Although mildly interested in photography for many years, it is only since joining Streatham CC in April 1993 that Aysen has taken a serious interest. She writes, "Whereas in the past I used to go out with a camera bag laden with a variety of lenses, Cokin filters and other gadgets, I now take only my camera and standard lens, enjoying the self-imposed discipline of concentrating on the subject itself and the composition of the shot." *(155, 157)*

Vivienne M Smith LRPS *(Hertfordshire)*
On the day Vivienne submitted her entry for this book, she heard that she had been awarded her Licentiateship of the RPS. Getting her first slr in 1989, she has progressed through a photography course for beginners to completing a City & Guilds course. Vivienne's main subject interests include nature, portrait and landscape, "but these are constantly changing as I get new inspiration". *(49, 97)*

Mark Snowdon *(North Yorkshire)*
Mark developed his interest in photography in 1986 whilst living in South Africa. He works almost entirely in monochrome, normally using medium format cameras, with a preferred combination of Agfa APX25 film and Rodinal developer. He became an Associate of the RPS in 1991 and is currently working towards the Fellowship. *(154)*

Ray Spence *(Warwickshire)*
Ray's passion for photography was kindled while taking a degree in microbiology and, after a 12 year stint as a biology teacher, he changed his career to become Head of Photography at Solihull College. He is a Fellow of the Royal Photographic Society and has lectured and exhibited widely in the UK. In 1994, Creative Monochrome published a portfolio of his work, *Form & Fantasy*. *(12)*

David Swailes *(Tyne & Wear)*
(35)

David Thorne *(Norfolk)*
David has been making photographic images for his own enjoyment for many years, and is now beginning to share them with a wider audience. He has staged two exhibitions in the last year and is now aiming towards publication. He acknowledges a particular debt to Barry Thornton for his help and guidance. His main subject interest is landscape, although he often prefers to concentrate on details rather than wide vistas. *(61)*

George E Todd *(Germany)*
George describes himself as a fugitive from colour photography. He has, in fact, built a distinguished reputation as a colour worker, with exhibitions around the world. Thus he is still uncertain whether his recent monochrome work is a temporary defection or a more permanent love affair. Now retired in the Bavarian village where he settled 21 years ago, he has a small lab/atelier and occasionally teaches photography in further education centres, and he says he would welcome the opportunity to help others in his English mother tongue. *(13-16, 30, 158)*

Cliff Tweats *(Northumberland)*
Cliff took up photography about 40 years ago to record his family growing up. On being made redundant 10 years later, he started a wedding photography and portrait business which thrived for many years. His photography is now for pleasure rather than profit and he says that he mainly takes "gloomy landscapes". He gained his Associateship of the RPS during his retirement. *(3)*

Joe Tymkow LRPS *(Avon)*
The wildlife he saw while enjoying fishing trips encouraged Joe to buy a camera. He went to the local camera club "for a couple of weeks" to find out how to use it. That was 16 years ago, and he is still a member of Keynsham CC. He has since completed a City & Guilds course and gained his LRPS by submission. *(10, 87)*

Dr Chris Wainwright FRPS *(Berkshire)*
Chris joined the RPS in 1975, gaining his Fellowship in 1982, and is now a member of the Society's Council. He is President of Bracknell CC and a founder member of the Arena group. A well known lecturer, judge and exhibitor, he was invited in 1989 to give a lecture tour in Hong Kong. He is the author of *The Creative Darkroom Handbook*, published in 1994 by Cassell. *(160)*

Brian C Walker *(Wiltshire)*
Brian is a commercial, industrial and wedding photographer, who has also been teaching photography in Swindon for several years. In 1993 his past and present students staged an exhibition in the Link Centre Library, Swindon, and another is being held in 1994 at the request

of the Chief Librarian. Brian is an Associate of the RPS and has had his images published in a number of photographic magazines. *(40, 72)*

Darren Warner *(London)*
Darren has been taking photographs for 12 years. He has a passion for the landscape and the majority of his personal and commissioned work has been in this area. He has completed a project, Wood, Water, Rock – a personal view of the Welsh landscape and its legends, which has already been exhibited in three locations. *(108)*

Paul Warner *(Worcestershire)*
Paul is a photographer and sculptor who is using his work to "explore thresholds within myself and the world as I experience it". Because of this, and the multiple layers of understanding which he intends in his images, he finds titles for his images unhelpful. He admits that many of his images perplex him: "I find you can explore without knowing what you are going to find". *(74, 75, 151)*

Philip Warren *(Northumberland)*
Actively involved in photography since his schooldays, Philip particularly enjoys landscape photography. He works mainly with medium format equipment in monochrome, processing and printing his own work. He gained his Licentiateship of the RPS in 1991 and hopes to achieve his Associateship "eventually". *(50, 86)*

Nick Warwick *(East Sussex)*
(20)

Harry Weekers *(Herefordshire)*
Harry has been taking photographs for 30 years, but has recently concentrated on what he describes as "narrative portraiture", finding India to be the ideal place for this work. He gained his Associateship of the RPS in 1972 and has had images accepted in national and international exhibitions. *(26, 27)*

Tim West *(West Sussex)*
Tim's photography is purely for pleasure, covering a wide range of subjects, although with a particular interest in motor racing. He tries to keep his camera and printing techniques as simple as possible. He has been a member of Midhurst CC for 17 years and is an active member of the Contemporary group of the RPS, gaining his Associateship in 1989. *(19)*

Colin Westgate *(East Sussex)*
Colin has been making photographs for 35 years, most of that time as a member of Eastbourne PS. He is a member of the London Salon, the Arena Group, and UPP, and holds the MFIAP and FRPS distinctions. He now organises and runs workshops for both monochrome and colour photography. *(116)*

Jean Wheeler *(Hampshire)*
An exhibition several years ago at The Barbican of Ansel Adams's work inspired Jean to join a course on monochrome photography: "being able to see the whole process through, from putting the film in the camera to hanging the photograph on the wall, has great appeal". Jean is a member of Image Workshop and of Winchester Photographic Society. *(96)*

David G Wilding LRPS *(Gwent)*
David gained his Licentiateship of the RPS in 1988 by direct submission, whilst studying the modular City & Guilds course in photography. He has had many acceptances in national and international exhibitions and some of his images have been published in magazines. He held a solo exhibition in Cwmbran in 1991 and has another scheduled in Gwent this year. *(17)*

Andy Wilson *(Nottinghamshire)*
Andy is a Friend of, and exhibitor in, the London Salon of Photography, and has acceptances in many national and international exhibitions. He is a founder member of the Triangle group of fine art monochrome printer/ photographers and has had his images published in several photographic magazines. Andy is also a judge and lecturer on the local club circuit. *(73, 116)*

Ken Wilson *(East Sussex)*
Although given his first camera some 60 years ago, it was not until he joined Southwick CC five or six years ago that he began to take a serious interest in photography. His main subject interest is landscape photography. Ken has had a number of successes in club competitions and hopes to win the trophy in the Club's annual exhibition: he was joint winner in 1994. *(84)*

Sandy Wilson *(Hampshire)*
Sandy is interested in all aspects of photography, but his main subjects currently are landscapes and church interiors. He belongs to a local camera club, where he enjoys helping other members to progress their photography. *(58, 63)*

Bill Wisden *(East Sussex)*
Bill is a well known lecturer to photographic societies, spending much of his time encouraging others that "all is possible". A Fellow of the RPS, Associate of the PAGB, and a member of the London Salon, Bill is the chairman of the RPS Pictorial distinctions panel. *(90)*

Dudley Woods ARPS *(Warwickshire)*
A photographer and writer, Dudley has been taking photographs for 20 years. His work has been exhibited in national salons and reproduced as posters. He prints his own images and strives to produce photographs with mood and atmosphere. He is currently working on a project, Ancient Stones, about the inspirational influence of Britain's prehistoric past. *(4, 5)*

Voting for the BoF awards

The images in *Best of Friends* are the equivalent of an exhibition of Friends' work. As is customary in such exhibitions, there will be awards for a small number of prints which especially capture the judges' attention. All Friends of Creative Monochrome are invited to be the judges and to cast votes to determine the award winners.

Here's what to do. Each Friend has a maximum of 10 votes to cast. Within that limit, you may award the votes as you see fit. For example, you could choose 10 prints to give one vote each; or you could give all 10 votes to one image; or somewhere in between. Votes can only be used in whole numbers. Friends may not vote for their own work.

To vote, for each image selected, write down the image number (*not* the page number), photographer and number of votes awarded. Please also include your own name and address (or membership number). Send your vote to: Creative Monochrome Ltd, 20 St Peters Road, Croydon, Surrey, CR0 1HD, England, **to arrive by 28 February 1995**. Alternatively, you can send your vote by fax to 081-681 0662.

Glossary of abbreviations used in profiles

AMPA Associate of the Master Photographers Association

BPE British Photographic Exhibitor – starred awards depending on acceptances in recognised national exhibitions

CC Camera Club

FIAP (*translated as*) International Federation of Photographic Art: awards distinctions of Associate, Exhibitor and Master, based on acceptances in recognised international exhibitions

FIPF Fellow of the Irish Photographic Federation

PS Photographic Society

PSA Photographic Society of America

RPS The Royal Photographic Society (UK): awards distinctions at Licentiate, Associate and Fellowship levels, primarily by submission of work for assessment by admissions panels

slr Single lens reflex: a type of camera using a prism and mirror to allow the photographer to view the subject through the camera lens

UPP United Photographic Postfolios.

Friends of Creative Monochrome

Membership of Friends of Creative Monochrome is open to everyone who enjoys monochrome photography, whether an active photographer or not, and shares the desire to see new work published. It is not restricted to any particular type or style of monochrome photography and is open to photographers of all ability levels, from beginner to seasoned professional.

Membership is free of charge: there is no annual subscription and no requirement to buy books (although we obviously hope you will!).

Members receive a free quarterly newsletter, special pre-publication offers on new books, the opportunity to buy signed copies of selected books, the chance to submit work for *Best of Friends*, prize draws and many other benefits.

To join, or to request further information, please write to:

Creative Monochrome Ltd
20 St Peters Road, Croydon, Surrey, CR0 1HD, England.

or telephone 081-686 3282 or fax 081-681 0662.

Data Protection Act: Friends' details are stored on computer for the sole use of Creative Monochrome Ltd; these details are not sold, rented or lent in any form to third parties for any purpose.